I HAVE AN EATING DISORDER.

NOW WHAT?

KRISTI LEW

ROSEN PUBLISHING®

New York

Published in 2015 by The Rosen Publishing Group, Inc.
29 East 21st Street, New York, NY 10010

Library of Congress Cataloging-in-Publication Data

Lew, Kristi, author.
I have an eating disorder. Now what?/Kristi Lew.—
First edition.
    pages cm.—(Teen life 411)
Includes bibliographical references and index.
ISBN 978-1-4777-7972-9 (library bound)
1. Eating disorders in adolescence—Juvenile literature.
2. Eating disorders—Causes—Juvenile literature. 3. Eating
disorders—Treatment—Juvenile literature. I. Title. II. Series:
Teen life 411.
RC552.E18L52 2015
616.85'26—dc23
                                                    2014007762

Manufactured in China

CONTENTS

Think about the last meal you ate. How do these thoughts make you feel? If the thought of eating makes you anxious, ashamed, or frightened, you may have an eating disorder.

People with eating disorders are controlled by their obsessive thoughts about food and weight, often to the exclusion of everything else. If they don't receive professional help, this intense focus on food can have a devastating effect on their physical and psychological health, their personal relationships, and their academic performance.

According to the National Eating Disorders Association (NEDA), approximately twenty million American women and ten million American men have struggled with an eating disorder. These numbers may be underestimated, however, because not everyone who has an eating disorder seeks treatment.

Adolescents appear to be more at risk for developing an eating disorder than the general population. Statistics gathered by the National Association of Anorexia Nervosa and Associated Disorders (ANAD) indicates that 95 percent of people with eating disorders are between the ages of twelve and twenty-five. In fact, eating disorders are now the third most commonly diagnosed chronic illness in adolescent girls (with asthma and obesity being numbers one and two, respectively).

Because of the ways in which eating disorders are often portrayed in the media, many people may be under the false impression that eating disorders affect

Constant worry about weight gain or weight loss may be a symptom of a developing eating disorder. With professional help, people who suffer from eating disorders can develop a healthy relationship with food and weight.

only wealthy, teenaged, white females. In reality, at least 5 to 15 percent of the people suffering from eating disorders are male, and the illness can affect people of any age, race, gender, or socioeconomic class.

Having an eating disorder is not a weakness. Nor are eating disorders diets, lifestyle choices, fads, or phases. People who slightly restrict their calorie intake in order to lose a few pounds probably do not have an eating disorder. Nor do people who occasionally give into the desire to eat too much of their favorite food. Picky eaters and those who have a "sweet tooth" generally do not have eating disorders either. People who suffer from an eating disorder feel an overwhelming, uncontrollable compulsion to continue a disordered pattern of eating, even when they realize that the behavior is unhealthy and self-destructive.

Although eating disorders are characterized by obsessive thoughts about food and weight, these disorders are not really about either of these things. Instead, the misuse and abuse of food are generally symptoms of underlying emotional issues. These issues may include self-hatred, depression, or feeling lost, alone, or out of control. Sufferers often feel powerless in the face of these uncomfortable emotions and get trapped into unhealthy eating habits in an attempt to cope with their emotional pain. Unfortunately, instead of alleviating the pain, the eating disorder only worsens it.

An eating disorder can lead to feelings of shame, despair, and loneliness. It can divert time and energy away from friends, family, and activities that were once enjoyed. An eating disorder also puts the victim's physical and mental health at risk. Sufferers may experience overwhelming feelings of anxiety and fear, even as they are recovering. They may fear that they are harming their bodies. Most of all, they fear that they will never be able to change their eating habits.

If you have an eating disorder, there are a few things you should know: You do not need to face these fears alone. Eating disorders are treatable and recovery is possible. With help, you can learn to have a healthy relationship with food and your body.

CHAPTER 1

WHAT IS AN EATING DISORDER?

While all eating disorders are characterized by an unhealthy relationship with food and weight, doctors and psychologists have identified several different types. Each type of eating disorder manifests itself in a different way, although some symptoms may overlap. People who have struggled with one type of eating disorder are often susceptible to developing a different one at a later date.

ANOREXIA NERVOSA

Anorexia is a Greek word that means "loss of appetite." *Nervosa* comes from Latin and means "for nervous reasons." Anorexia nervosa is an eating disorder that is characterized by self-starvation and extreme weight loss.

Despite its name, people suffering from anorexia nervosa do not really lose their appetite. Instead, they are so terrified of gaining weight that they learn to ignore the signs and symptoms of hunger and refuse to eat. Eventually, they become so malnourished and lose so much weight that they suffer a variety of health problems, which may include death.

Research indicates that adolescents, especially adolescent girls, have a higher risk of developing an eating disorder than adults.

Although anorexia can strike at any age, difficulty with the disorder often begins in puberty when the body naturally begins to fill out. Even though this is a natural process that happens to every adolescent, people who develop anorexia perceive this weight gain as alarming. The development of anorexia may also occur in response to a physical attack or psychological bullying. People who suffer from the disorder may feel that school or personal relationships have become overwhelming.

Outwardly, people with anorexia tend to be good students, well behaved, and eager to please. They are often perfectionists. Inwardly, however, they may experience feelings of anxiousness, loneliness, depression, or insecurity.

Anorexia often begins with something as simple as going on a diet to lose a few extra pounds. However, for people who develop anorexia, this diet gradually gets more and more restrictive as time goes on. Eventually, they develop a habit of obsessively counting every calorie in the foods that they consume and repeatedly weighing themselves to make sure they have not gained any weight. When other people notice and admire their weight loss, they may feel vindicated and validated to continue their self-destructive habits.

People with anorexia often develop rules about what, when, where, and with whom they will eat. If you find yourself applying strict rules and rituals to mealtimes and certain foods, you may be in danger of developing anorexia.

Eating disorders can affect anyone anywhere, but those in the public eye can be especially vulnerable. Being rich and famous does not prevent people from struggling with eating disorders. In fact, it often exacerbates the problem.

Anorexia nervosa and other eating disorders were first brought to the widespread attention of the public when musician Karen Carpenter died of heart failure in 1983. She was thirty-two years old. After being called "chubby" in a magazine article, the twenty-four-year-old singer secretly descended into what would ultimately become a fatal struggle with anorexia.

Carpenter is not the only celebrity to have difficulty finding a balance between living in the public eye and managing a personal struggle. Royals, such as Princess Diana of Wales and Princess Victoria, the Crown Princess of Sweden, have spoken publicly about their battles with eating disorders. So have the popular singers Paula Abdul and Geri Halliwell (better known as Ginger Spice of the Spice Girls). Abdul and Halliwell have both gotten help for their eating disorders and are living much healthier lives today.

Other celebrities who have fought with various eating disorders include Christina Ricci, Mary-Kate Olsen, Lindsay Lohan, Tracey Gold, Jamie-Lynn Sigler, and Billy Bob Thornton. Daniel Johns, Fiona Apple, and Elton John have waged their own battles. Many others, including contemporary pop artist Kesha, realize the danger of struggling alone and choose to undergo formal treatment.

FOCUSING ATTENTION ON EATING DISORDERS

According to the NEDA, 90 to 95 percent of people with anorexia are girls and women. In fact, anorexia has become one of the most commonly diagnosed psychiatric illnesses in adolescent girls. It also has one of the highest mortality risks of any psychiatric disorder. Statistics state that 5 to 20 percent of the people who develop anorexia will die of the disease. The risk of death increases with the length of time the person has suffered from the illness.

BINGE EATING DISORDER

Binge eating disorder is characterized by the uncontrollable urge to eat large amounts of food. Some people who suffer from binge eating disorder rapidly consume excessive amounts of calories in short bursts. Others report eating almost constantly. People struggling with this disorder often hoard food, eat in secret, and hide the evidence of what they have eaten. Many sufferers report being obsessed with food. They spend enormous amounts of time either thinking about it or eating it. This disorder may also be called compulsive overeating.

Everyone overindulges every now and then, whether it is at Thanksgiving dinner or accidentally polishing off a bag of chips while watching television. Unlike the occasional episode of overeating, however, someone with binge eating disorder has little or no control over his or her eating patterns. Binge eating disorder sufferers may eat normally in front of others and then again when they are alone. They may also eat to the point of pain but feel powerless to stop themselves.

Some celebrities, including Lindsay Lohan, have publicly acknowledged their struggles with eating disorders.

People who suffer from binge eating disorder eat whether they feel hungry or not. They are not trying to assuage hunger but to ease emotional tension. When not left alone or when prevented from eating, they may feel angry and anxious. The disorder is often associated with depression as well.

People with binge eating disorder may counter the calories they eat with exercise. As a consequence, they may be of normal weight or just slightly overweight. However, many people who suffer from binge eating disorder are obese.

According to the Binge Eating Disorder Association (BEDA), binge eating is the most common eating disorder in the United States. Unlike anorexia, which predominantly affects females, binge eating disorder afflicts nearly as many men as it does women. The NEDA reports that about 60 percent of people suffering from binge eating disorder are female and 40 percent are male.

Bulimia Nervosa

Bulimia nervosa is an eating disorder characterized by periods of binge eating followed by purging. Purging, in this context, means the removal of food from the body, by means of self-induced vomiting after eating, for example, or the elimination of calories consumed after the fact. Many people believe that if they do not intentionally throw up after meals they cannot have bulimia. However, people suffering from bulimia may

How do you know if you have an eating disorder? Do you ever feel as if people would like you more if you were just a little bit thinner? Do you ever find yourself thinking about food or how to avoid it to the exclusion of everything else? These thoughts and feelings may be a warning sign that an eating disorder is developing.

People with low self-esteem who do not feel that they are as worthy or attractive as those around them may be in danger of developing an eating disorder. People with false ideas of what their body actually looks like may be in danger, too. For example, if you are constantly receiving comments about how thin you are but you still feel fat, you may have a distorted body image. People with distorted body images perceive their own bodies differently from the way others see them or how they actually are.

Warning signs in young men may be slightly different from those in young women. Where girls tend to obsess about overall weight loss or gain, boys tend to choose a specific body part to dwell on. They may, for example, exercise obsessively or drink nutritional supplements in the pursuit of rock-hard abs or a broader chest.

If you find yourself becoming preoccupied with food, your weight, calories, exercise, or dieting, it may be time to talk to a trusted adult.

WARNING SIGNS

purge in other ways, including the abuse of diuretics or laxatives, compulsive over-exercising, or alternating episodes of binge eating with periods of fasting.

Like anorexia, bulimia often appears for the first time during puberty. Also like anorexia, bulimia affects a higher percentage of females than males. According to the NEDA, 80 percent of bulimia sufferers are young women.

Bulimia also has some traits in common with binge eating disorder. People who suffer from bulimia are often very secretive. They may hide stockpiles of food and conceal the evidence of their binges by burying food wrappers at the bottom of the garbage can or secretively cleaning up dirty dishes.

Although people with bulimia may be as terrified of gaining weight as someone with anorexia, they do not tend to be abnormally thin. They may, in fact, be slightly overweight. This is often the case when the amount of calories a person suffering from bulimia consumes during binges exceeds the amount of calories that he or she is able to purge. Because of this, a person suffering from bulimia may be harder to identify than someone struggling with anorexia.

Compulsive overeating may be a symptom of either binge eating disorder or bulimia. The difference between the two disorders is that people with bulimia have an overwhelming need to purge after eating excessive calories.

People with bulimia often feel so ashamed, frightened, or disgusted by their binging habits that they feel an overwhelming need to purge. While people with anorexia often deny that they have a problem, those suffering from bulimia may realize that their relationship with food is unhealthy and they keep the problem a secret. This secrecy often increases the unwanted emotions that lead to the compulsion to binge and purge, resulting in a never-ending, vicious cycle. However, like most other eating disorders, the chances of recovery increase with early intervention.

Other Eating Disorders

Some people may have a handful of the symptoms of anorexia or bulimia, but they

People with bulimia often experience an overwhelming need to purge after eating. They may also experience a crushing sense of shame over their inability to control their actions.

do not exactly fit the diagnosis of either disorder. They may, for example, purge without binging or they may chew food but then spit it out. No matter how they eat or do not eat, these disorders, like anorexia, bulimia, and binge eating, are still characterized by emotional and psychological pain when dealing with issues of food, weight, or body image. Doctors and psychologists refer to these disorders as eating disorders not otherwise specified, or EDNOS.

There are also named eating disorders that are much less common than anorexia, bulimia, or binge eating disorder. These disorders include pica, night-eating disorder, Prader-Willi syndrome, anorexia athletica, diabulimia, and orthorexia nervosa. Pica is the uncontrollable urge to eat non-food items, such as dirt, chalk, clay, coins, or soap. A person with night-eating disorder binge eats while sleepwalking. Prader-Willi syndrome is a genetic disorder. One of its symptoms is the compulsive urge to binge eat.

Anorexia athletica is also called compulsive exercising disorder. People who have this disorder exercise obsessively to lose weight. Anorexia athletica may be found in conjunction with other eating disorders.

Diabulimia is an extremely dangerous eating disorder that affects people with type 1 diabetes. A person suffering from diabulimia deliberately takes less insulin than his or her body needs in order to lose weight.

Engaging in extremely long exercise sessions may be a symptom of a developing eating disorder, especially anorexia athletica.

Orthorexia nervosa is an unhealthy obsession with "healthy" eating. People who suffer from orthorexia nervosa are fixated on food quality and purity. This disorder may start out as a healthy desire to eat organic or high-quality foods. Eventually, however, the obsession to eat only what are perceived to be the "right" foods leads to such restrictive food choices that the person's health suffers.

If you are concerned about your eating habits or body image, you owe it to yourself and your family and friends to speak to a health professional about your concerns whether you fit into one of these categories or not.

Scientists have not yet identified a specific, individual cause of eating disorders. Instead, doctors and psychologists have observed that these disorders seem to develop for a variety of reasons. Health care professionals have identified some contributing factors, however. These factors include body chemistry, psychological stress, and societal pressure. In reality, the reasons that eating disorders develop and persist are usually due to a combination of these factors.

BIOLOGICAL CAUSES

Scientific studies have revealed that, in some people, eating disorders may have a genetic link. Researchers observe that people who live in families with a history of eating disorders, anxiety disorders, or depression seem to have a higher risk of developing these conditions themselves. Experts have noticed that perfectionism and compulsions tend to run in families, too. These traits may also contribute to the development of an eating disorder. Scientists are unsure how much the development of an eating disorder is due to genetics and how much is a result of learned behavior.

Researchers have also found that particular chemicals in the brain and body may be

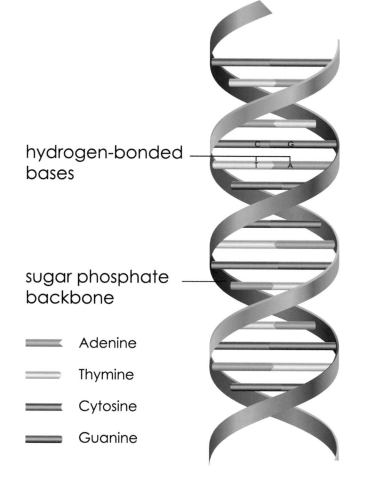

hydrogen-bonded bases

sugar phosphate backbone

Adenine

Thymine

Cytosine

Guanine

The makeup of our DNA controls more than we can often identify. Scientists now believe that genetics may play a larger part in the development of an eating disorder than they previously thought.

unbalanced in some people with eating disorders. For example, scientists have discovered that people who develop anorexia often have higher levels of a hormone called cortisol than people who do not have anorexia. Cortisol is released during periods of stress. One of its effects is to suppress appetite by inhibiting a chemical called neuropeptide Y. Doctors believe this may be one of the reasons why people with anorexia limit their food intake in response to stress.

Researchers have also found that, compared to people who do not have an eating disorder, people with anorexia and bulimia often tend to have higher concentrations of a brain chemical called serotonin. Serotonin is a neurotransmitter that helps regulate mood. The implications of higher serotonin levels and how it may contribute to the onset and perpetuation of an eating disorder is still being researched.

Other chemicals in the body, called leptin and ghrelin, regulate the appetite. Leptin is a hormone released by fat cells that decreases appetite. Ghrelin is released primarily by the stomach, and scientists believe that it may signal hunger in the brain. An imbalance between these two hormones may have ramifications for many people who suffer from a variety of eating disorders.

Doctors do not believe that chemical imbalances in the brain and body alone cause a person to develop an eating disorder. Instead, they think that if a chemical imbalance exists alongside other conditions, such as stress or trauma, the chemical imbalance may put

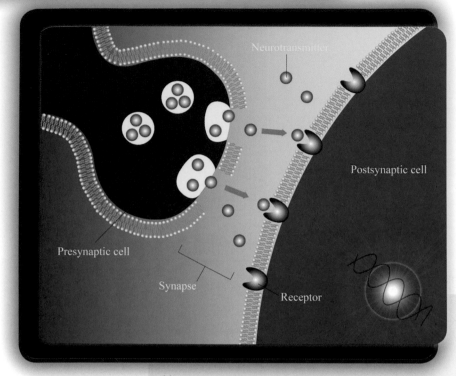

Neurotransmitter

Postsynaptic cell

Presynaptic cell

Synapse

Receptor

Neurotransmitters, such as serotonin, communicate information throughout the brain and body. An imbalance in these chemicals may trigger symptoms such as depression, trouble sleeping, and cravings for certain foods.

an individual at a higher risk of developing an eating disorder. They do know that as an eating disorder progresses it commonly causes chemical imbalances in the body to increase, possibly perpetuating the illness. Using these findings and additional ongoing studies, scientists hope one day to develop more comprehensive medical and therapeutic strategies to help people who suffer from eating disorders.

PSYCHOLOGICAL CAUSES

Doctors have found that eating disorders are typically triggered by emotional stress. Their onset often occurs in conjunction with periods of major change. Contributing factors may include the problems or arguing at home due to divorce, drug abuse, alcoholism, or physical, emotional, or sexual abuse. Coping with a family member's health problems or death, moving to a new town, changing schools, going off to college, breaking up with a boyfriend or girlfriend, a broken friendship, or another traumatic event can also result in the emotional turmoil that can trigger the beginnings of an eating disorder.

Oftentimes, people who struggle with an eating disorder try to use food to fulfill an emotional, rather than a physical, need. They may feel as if their life is out of control or they may feel awkward or out of place among family, friends, and classmates. They may turn to food for comfort or feel as though restricting their food intake is a way to exert control over part of their lives.

For athletes, an eating disorder may start out as a desire to please a coach by losing weight for a particular sport. A comment about weight or body shape delivered by a friend or family member may also lead a susceptible person down the dangerous path to an eating disorder. Others may use food to ease loneliness or to avoid difficult feelings associated with particular memories.

People who develop eating disorders may also be struggling with depression or low self-esteem. Most

people with eating disorders are smart and caring. They feel deeply for the people around them and they want to please them. Many tend to be perfectionists as well. A person battling an eating disorder often wants to do the right thing. This type of person has what is known as "black and white thinking." As a consequence, in his or her head, a person with an eating disorder perceives his or her own body as either right or wrong and certain foods as either good or bad. There is no in-between.

People who suffer from an eating disorder are often trying to bring some sense of control or happiness into their lives and they believe that mastering their eating

Tension and stress at home may trigger or exacerbate the struggle with an eating disorder. Very often, an eating disorder provides a false sense of control in an otherwise unstable environment.

habits will help them accomplish this. Sometimes, focusing on their appearance allows people with eating disorders to avoid deeper, more complicated issues, too. Unfortunately, an eating disorder tends to makes matters worse and somebody who was already feeling overwhelmed, sad, or anxious will end up even more overwhelmed than before the eating disorder took hold.

Body Image

People who suffer from an eating disorder have particular difficulty accepting their bodies the way that they are. They often feel that if they were thinner, they would fit in better or that people would like them more. They see themselves as imperfect and are determined to do whatever they can to manage and control these imperfections.

For some, this means trying to make themselves more attractive to others by losing weight. For others, their eating disorders are not prompted by appearance as much as the desire to be the best, or the most fit, at a sport. Athletic endeavors that have weight restrictions—such as gymnastics, dance, horseback riding, swimming, track, wrestling, and rowing—may propel someone into disordered eating.

People with some eating disorders have a very skewed image of what their bodies actually look like to

Certain sports, such as gymnastics and wrestling, have weight restrictions. With some people, the struggle to maintain what is considered to be the "perfect" weight for these sports may cause them to develop disordered eating habits.

others. Someone who has anorexia, for example, may be little more than skin and bones, and yet that person would still say that he or she feels fat. This is an example of a distorted body image. Body image is how you think you appear to other people. This mental picture may or may not have any basis whatsoever in reality.

People with eating disorders may try to camouflage what they feel is an imperfect body by wearing baggy, oversized clothes. They often compare their weight or body shape to others, especially to unattainable idolized shapes of people they see in the media. A slightly different, but related, disorder, called body dysmorphic disorder, may appear in conjunction with an eating disorder. People with body dysmorphic disorder tend to obsess over a particular body part that they feel is misshapen or ugly, even when it is perfectly healthy. Many of the same underlying causes that affect people with eating disorders also affect those with body dysmorphic disorder.

In fact, body dissatisfaction appears to be the number one contributor to the development of an eating disorder. That being the case, the NEDA reports some disturbing statistics about the attitudes of elementary school girls toward weight and body size. According to the NEDA, girls as young as six years old express concern about their weight. About half of these first graders were afraid of getting too fat. Experts are unsure whether these negative attitudes are learned at home or initiated by social contact. Most likely, a combination of factors is involved. Negative body image or "fat shaming" comments from friends or family members that criticize weight can easily influence someone with an underlying genetic, psychological, or environmental predisposition toward developing an eating disorder to tip over the edge into unhealthy eating behaviors.

SOCIAL AND SOCIETAL CAUSES

People today are constantly bombarded with images from television, advertisements, and the Internet. The images of beautiful, thin people who seem to have it all can be quite overwhelming. Young women often feel pressure from society to be thin. Young men are not immune to that pressure either; it just takes a different form. Instead of the need to be thin, young men often feel the pressure to be physically fit and athletically powerful.

The perception of the ideal body shape differs depending on when and where you are born. In the Middle Ages, for example, larger, plump bodies were considered more desirable than thin, lean forms because it meant that the heavier person was wealthy and well fed. Even today, curvaceous bodies are widely considered more desirable in some societies and cultures than in others. In cultures that promote relatively heavier weights and larger body sizes, eating disorders are much less common than in other cultures, such as contemporary European or American cultures, which tend to idolize thinness.

Placing too much emphasis on thinness can have negative consequences for everyone, but especially for teenaged girls. The bodies of pubescent teenagers are growing and changing rapidly. For this process to occur healthily, their bodies need the proper nutrition. The inability to reach the level of thinness seen in models can cause disappointment and depression, possibly triggering a bout with an eating disorder.

The images that people see in the media can alter their perception of what is normal. Not all bodies are as thin as those shown on television or in advertisements. And, they are not supposed to be. All bodies have different sizes and shapes, and they grow and develop at different rates. Even celebrities featured on the cover of magazines are not always happy with the ways that they are portrayed. According to an article in the *Huffington Post*, actress Kate Winslet thought her picture on the cover of the February 2003 issue of *GQ* magazine was subjected to too much manipulation. "The retouching is excessive. I do not look like that and more importantly I don't desire to look like that," Winslet said.

Every year, Americans spend billions of dollars on diets, diet aids, and gym memberships in the quest to lose weight. Advertisers take advantage of this desire to be thinner by attempting to convince people that the newest celebrity diet, diet soda, or exercise center will be the answer to all of their problems. The media is not

Despite what some social networking groups might have you believe, anorexia and bulimia are not lifestyle choices; they are dangerous disorders. People in online groups that promote anorexia or bulimia are often suffering from eating disorders themselves and are seeking justification for their out-of-control habits. Unfortunately, in doing so they perpetuate harmful images and ideas that they misleadingly label "thinspiration." Two hoaxes promoted by several social media platforms that have fooled a lot of people include the so-called "thigh gap" and "bikini bridge." The thigh gap is allegedly attained by becoming so thin that your thighs do not touch even when you stand with your feet together. A bikini bridge is supposedly the gap that forms between the strap on bikini bottoms and a girl's abdomen by her protruding hipbones when she lies down. Both are considerably unhealthy and unattainable weight loss goals, and the bikini bridge is an out-and-out lie. According to *E! Online*, a user on the imageboard website 4chan invented the bikini bridge with the sole intention of creating a trend that would go viral. What the uninitiated do not realize is that groups who promote "thinspiration" purposefully produce highly manipulated images, profess to offer support in an incredibly negative manner, and teach decidedly destructive practices. If you believe you may be suffering from an eating disorder, these sites do not, as they say, offer help. In fact, they are inconceivably toxic, and it is best to stay away from them.

EATING DISORDERS AND SOCIAL MEDIA

the only pressure people may encounter, however. Friends may bond by commiserating with each other about how fat they feel or how much they want to lose weight. Family members may do this as well. Parents who are consistently dieting may encourage their children to diet, too.

For many years, experts blamed media images for an increase in eating disorders at the beginning of the twentieth century. Today, they no longer believe that the media alone causes eating disorder. However, it does appear to strongly contribute to them.

Self-Esteem

Low self-esteem is very common in people with

Magazines and other media outlets tend to focus on a specific body type, often tall and thin, creating unrealistic expectations in the young men and women who are routinely exposed to these images.

eating disorders. Self-esteem is a feeling of satisfaction with one's achievements, appearance, and abilities. Over time, the approval and encouragement given by family and friends increases a person's self-esteem. Negative feedback, on the other hand, can have harmful, long-lasting effects. Parents with unrealistic expectations, classmates who bully, or friends who criticize and compare can damage self-esteem. People with high self-esteem, or a positive image of themselves, are much less likely than people with low self-esteem to develop an eating disorder.

Family dynamics not only help create or destroy a person's self-esteem but can also help form healthy or unhealthy eating habits and attitudes about food. People who grow up in families where food is seen as a reward, for example, may develop an eating disorder if they are trying to use food to re-create good, happy childhood memories. They may also dip into the world of eating disorders if low self-esteem makes them feel as if they are not worthy enough to get a "reward" and, therefore, deprive themselves of food.

Children whose parents severely restrict food choices—if they are worried about how unhealthy junk food and sodas are, for example—may later engage in secret binge eating of specific foods. Once in a while, this is not necessarily a problem, but in conjunction with other triggers, binge eating could spiral out of control and become a more harmful problem.

If someone in your family struggles with an eating disorder or body image issues, you should carefully consider monitoring your attitudes about food and eating. If you find your perspective on these matters shifting into obsessive thoughts about food or weight, speaking to a doctor or other health professional may help prevent the problem from spiraling out of control. Without help, eating disorders invariably lead to both physical and psychological harm. Getting help in the early stages can prevent permanent damage.

MYTHS AND FACTS

MYTH

People with anorexia do not get hungry.

FACT

People with anorexia are hungry much of the time. They have just trained themselves to ignore their body's hunger signals.

MYTH

Only young, wealthy, white girls struggle with eating disorders.

FACT

Anyone of any age, gender, race, and socioeconomic background can develop an eating disorder.

MYTH

All the health issues associated with an eating disorder will disappear once the person with the eating disorder is eating normally.

FACT

Damage to the heart, liver, kidneys, and reproductive system caused by an eating disorder may result in permanent physical harm.

MYTH

As long as I am not throwing up after every meal, I cannot have bulimia.

FACT

Not everyone with bulimia uses self-induced vomiting to purge. Some take laxatives, some exercise compulsively, and others alternate between overeating and fasting.

MYTH

You should not tell anyone that you have an eating disorder because people will think you are crazy.

FACT

Asking a trusted adult for help is actually one of the best things you can do. With their help, you can get the treatment you need to get healthy again.

CHAPTER 3

The human body needs nutrients to function properly. Nutrients are the chemical compounds in foods that the body uses to grow, fight disease, and make energy. They include carbohydrates, proteins, fats, vitamins, and minerals. To be healthy, people need to eat a balanced diet that includes all of these compounds.

HEALTH COMPLICATIONS

Severely restricting certain foods can throw the balance of nutrients off kilter. Binge eating has the same effect, but in a different way. Forcing food and water out of the body can also upset its normal functioning. In fact, any of these behaviors can have a devastating physical effect on the body. Sometimes, the damage cannot be undone.

Anorexia

There are a number of health complications associated with anorexia nervosa. Chief among them is the risk of death. You may recall that anorexia has the highest mortality risk of any psychiatric disorder and, according to the NEDA, 5 to 20 percent of the people who develop anorexia will die from the disease.

Because the body needs food to make energy, people with anorexia often feel tired and weak. They may pass out from the lack of calories or

CONSEQUENCES OF AN EATING DISORDER

suffer from frequent head-aches. The body needs nutrients to fuel the brain, too. Consequently, people with anorexia often find that they cannot concentrate very well and they may begin to have trouble at work or in school.

As the illness progresses, the digestive system slows down and sufferers may experience stomach and intestinal pain. The palms of the hands and soles of the feet may also turn yellow due to an imbalance in nutrient intake. In women, hormonal imbalances cause menstruation to become irregular and, eventually, to stop. The effects of anorexia on the reproductive system may or may not be reversible.

Eating disorders can have long-lasting effects, not only physically, but also academically, which may affect future opportunities. Low levels of nutrients can cause trouble with concentration or alertness in class.

As body fat disappears, so do its insulating properties. This lack of fat causes people with anorexia to feel cold all the time, even if the ambient temperature is quite warm. Eventually, a fine coating of hair, called lanugo, grows over the entire body in an effort to keep it warm. Fat also has a lubricating and moisturizing effect. Without it, the skin turns dry and flaky, and hair falls out.

It is not unusual for people who struggle with anorexia to develop osteoporosis, a condition in which the bones become brittle and are easily broken. According to the National Institutes of Health (NIH), studies have shown that people with anorexia may begin to incur bone loss relatively early in the progression of the illness. Several of the risk factors for developing osteoporosis overlap with the symptoms of anorexia. These risk factors include excessive thinness, amenorrhea (the absence of menstruation), and low calcium intake. In addition, people with anorexia sometimes try to ease their hunger by drinking massive amounts of diet soda, which can prevent the body from absorbing calcium. Because building healthy bones occurs during childhood and adolescence, the consequences of bone loss at this age can have disastrous lingering effects well into adulthood.

Denied of essential nutrients, the body is forced to slow down life-sustaining functions to conserve energy, often resulting in a slower heart rate and low blood pressure. As the heart rate slows, the danger of heart failure increases. When the body is not given

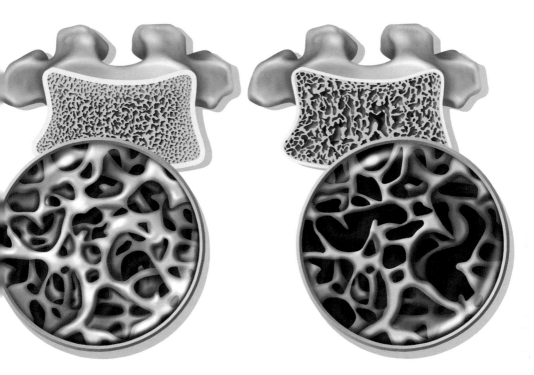

Bone health in adulthood relies on the accumulation of healthy bone mass *(top left)* during adolescence. If the body does not receive the proper nutrition during this critical phase of life, osteoporosis *(top right)* can result.

enough food to produce the energy it needs, it begins to break down muscle tissue, including the heart muscle. Mineral imbalances can also cause cardiac arrest, which may lead to permanent heart damage or death.

People with anorexia may limit their liquid intake as well as their ingestion of foods. Without food and beverages to provide the liquid that the body needs, dehydration can occur. Severe dehydration can lead to kidney damage, which may be irreversible. If the kidneys sustain permanent injury, dialysis may be required indefinitely for treatment.

Some people who suffer from anorexia may also engage in the practice of eating inedible materials, such as cotton balls soaked in juice. They believe that the cotton will act as a sponge and keep them from being hungry. Not only does this fail to stave off hunger, it is also an unhealthy practice. The body cannot digest cotton balls, and people who engage in this behavior risk creating an indigestible mass in the stomach or intestine. The only remedy for this situation is surgery. Without surgery to remove the blockage, the person may die.

Binge Eating Disorder

While severely restricting nutrient intake can have deadly consequences, so can binge eating. Binge eating destroys the body in different ways than anorexia, but it can be equally harmful and have long-lasting effects.

Some sufferers of eating disorders eat inedible objects, such as cotton balls, to feel full. Eating indigestible material, however, can result in serious and permanent injury.

Some people with binge eating disorder are over-weight, but many are obese. Obesity means having more body fat than is healthy. Being obese causes stress on the heart and circulatory system and can result in high blood pressure or coronary heart disease. The risk of developing type 2 diabetes also increases.

Eating foods high in saturated fats, such as meats, cheeses, butter, and most fried foods, increases the concentration of chemicals called triglycerides and low-density lipoproteins (LDL) in the blood. Low-density lipoproteins, along with their counterparts—high-density lipoproteins (HDL)—are commonly called cholesterol. Increased blood levels of triglycerides and LDL have been linked to coronary heart disease.

Coronary heart disease develops when a waxy sub-stance builds up inside the coronary arteries. This waxy buildup is called plaque and is made up of the triglycer-ides and LDL circulating in the blood. Coronary arteries supply oxygen-rich blood to the heart. If these arteries become blocked with plaque, the heart is deprived of oxygen and the person has a heart attack. If the blood flow is not quickly restored, the heart muscle begins to die. Without rapid treatment, this can lead to permanent heart damage or death.

Having type 2 diabetes can also put a person's health at risk. Type 2 diabetes develops when the body stops using insulin properly. Insulin is a hormone released by the pancreas that regulates the amount of glucose, or sugar, in the blood. In people with type 2 diabetes, the body cells have developed a resistance to insulin. This resistance causes a higher than normal blood glucose level, a condition called hyperglycemia. Having diabetes increases the risk of developing heart disease and high blood pressure, both of which increase the risk of having a heart attack. Hyperglycemia can also damage the eyes, nerves, and kidneys.

Some of the damage incurred by being obese can be reversed if the person loses weight. Many people with binge eating disorder try dieting to reduce their body fat, but then fall off the diet when the uncontrollable urge to eat returns. Unfortunately, a constant up and down pattern of weight can permanently change the way the body processes food, making it even harder to lose weight. However, with proper treatment, people with binge eating disorder can successfully change their eating habits and reset their metabolism.

Bulimia

Bulimia causes its own health problems. Like people with anorexia, people who suffer from bulimia often have nutrient and hormonal imbalances that cause irregular menstrual periods, amenorrhea, and osteoporosis. Repeated vomiting can also result in swollen salivary glands, making the cheeks look perpetually swollen. The force of esophageal contractions may also burst blood vessels in the eyes and face. Cuts on the fingers and knuckles are common when fingers are used to force vomiting.

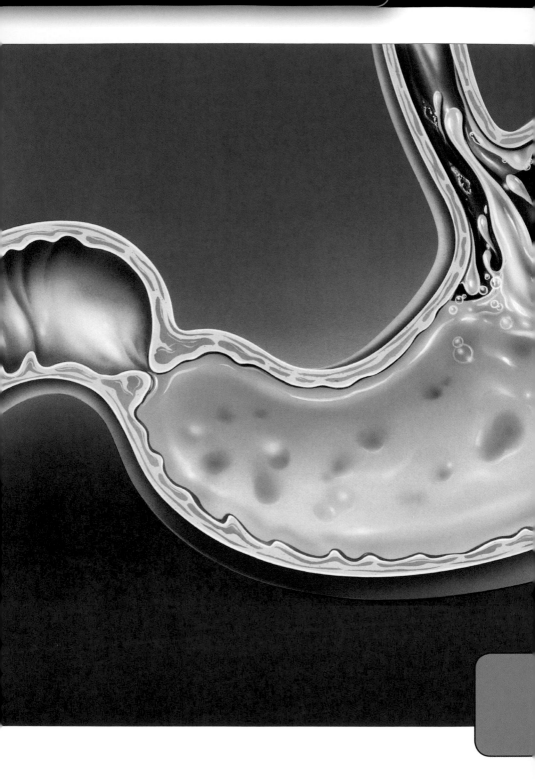

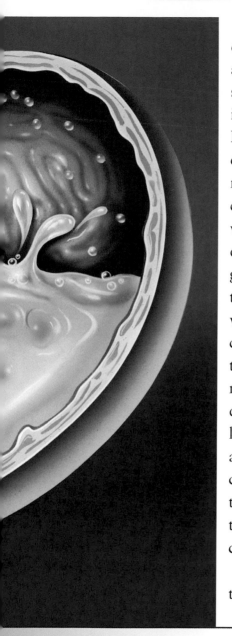

Stomach acid can also do massive amounts of damage. The stomach lining secretes gastric juices, which include hydrochloric acid. Hydrochloric acid is highly corrosive and would normally destroy human tissue on contact. A layer of mucus prevents the stomach from being digested, but the esophagus, gums, and teeth do not share this protective lining. Habitual vomiting can result in nearly constant heartburn, a sore throat, bleeding gums, and mouth ulcers. It can also break down tooth enamel, which leads to yellow, damaged teeth and tooth loss. Stomach acid can also erode or tear holes in the esophagus. In rare cases, the esophagus can rupture, causing sudden death.

Forced vomiting is not the only dangerous practice

Stomach acid is useful and necessary as long as it stays in the stomach. When it is forced up through the esophagus, however, it can cause extreme damage to the esophagus, gums, and teeth.

Athletes and Eating Disorders

It may seem counterintuitive, but people who engage in long-term excessive exercise, such as endurance training for marathon running, may be harming their hearts. According to the *Boston Globe*, mounting scientific evidence suggests that chronic overtraining is linked to irregular heartbeat and damage to the heart tissue, possibly due to the constant dilation and stretching of the heart's chambers.

Long distance runners are not the only ones at risk, though. People who exercise compulsively, either as an attempted antidote to binge eating or as part of anorexia athletica, may also suffer these consequences. Competing in certain sports may also encourage people with a predisposition toward developing an eating disorder to start down the wrong path. According to the NEDA, a study of Division 1 NCAA athletes showed that over one-third of the athletes had attitudes and feelings that would make them susceptible to developing anorexia nervosa.

Female athletes, in particular, are subject to a phenomenon called the female athlete triad. This condition is a combination of three health problems that often occur in conjunction in competitive female athletes. These health problems include disordered eating, amenorrhea, and the loss of bone mass.

Female athletes who compete in sports that emphasize weight and body shape, such as ice-skating, ballet, dance, or gymnastics, may be more susceptible to developing disordered eating than those who are involved in sports that promote fitness and strength, such as tennis or biking. Olympic gymnasts Cathy Rigby and Nadia

Comaneci, for example, have spoken publically of their battles with anorexia and bulimia. Twice, Rigby, who struggled with her eating disorder from 1968 to 1981, was rushed to the hospital while experiencing the same electrolyte imbalance that killed musician Karen Carpenter. But Rigby was luckier than Carpenter. She sought treatment and went on to a long and successful career as an actress and motivational speaker.

associated with bulimia. The overuse of laxatives or diuretics, chemicals designed to rid the body of water by promoting urine production, can also cause extensive damage. Fluid imbalances caused by laxative or diuretic use can lead to irregular bowel movements, resulting in constipation. Overuse of laxatives can also cause repeated diarrhea, which may lead to rectal prolapse. Rectal prolapse occurs when the rectum, the part of the colon just above the anus, stretches to the point that it protrudes from the anal opening. Abdominal or rectal surgery is usually necessary to repair the prolapse.

Laxatives work by drawing water out of body tissues and into the bowels, which can lead to dehydration. At best, dehydration causes headaches, dry skin, brittle nails, and hair loss. At worst, it can cause seizures, electrolyte imbalances, and death. Electrolytes are charged particles, or ions, that the body needs to function properly. Ions of potassium, for example, are necessary for

muscles, like the heart, to contract. The kidneys work to keep the electrolyte concentration in the blood balanced no matter how the chemistry of the body changes. Because the overuse of laxatives or diuretics can cause electrolyte imbalances, this practice may result in permanent kidney damage, muscle spasms, and heart irregularities, including cardiac arrest, which can lead to death.

EFFECTS ON MENTAL HEALTH AND RELATIONSHIPS

Many people with an eating disorder feel a lack of

The overuse of laxatives can cause electrolyte imbalances in the body, which may result in muscle spasms, permanent kidney damage, or heart attack.

control, shame, or defeat when it comes to their eating habits. These feelings can lead to emotional issues such as anxiety, depression, and stress. As a result, people who suffer with an eating disorder are at risk for suicide and substance abuse, both of which pose just as much of a risk to their health, if not more, than the eating disorder itself.

The emotional roller coaster and chemical imbalances in the body due to the lack of proper nutrition can affect personality, too, resulting in wide mood swings and a quick temper, which may alienate friends and family. As someone with an eating disorder becomes more and more focused on personal issues with food, that person will likely withdraw from family, friends, and activities that used to be of great interest, exacerbating feelings of loneliness and isolation. Someone who suffers from an eating disorder may also destroy other people's trust by sneaking away to purge, stealing food, or tricking people into thinking that he or she is eating more or less than is really the case. These actions sabotage relationships, which may be very difficult to repair or win back.

CHAPTER 4

Eating disorders rarely go away on their own, but there is help available. With professional knowledge, support, and proper medical care, an eating disorder can be overcome. Just as there is no specific cause for an eating disorder, there is no singular cure either. Recovery can be a long and complicated process, and several treatment plans may need to be pursued before finding the one that is right for the situation. However, breaking old habits and replacing them with healthier ones is possible and may prevent permanent harm to your body, psyche, and relationships.

ASKING FOR HELP

Asking for help and learning to reach out to others is not always easy. Often people with serious eating disorders deny that there is anything wrong and will not seek treatment on their own. Instead, an intervention by a friend, family member, or some other caring individual may be needed in order to save their lives.

People who have suffered from eating disorders in the past often report that admitting that they had a problem was one of the most difficult steps they had to take. However, they also report that they are very happy that they finally did so. All the energy people with eating disorders expend on controlling what they eat and how they eat it can be better spent on developing their unique personality and learning to live a happy, healthy life.

The thought of getting help may seem scary in the beginning. Some people feel as if an eating disorder is the only thing that makes them unique. If you suffer from an eating disorder, seeking help may feel like giving up a part of your identity. However, this is just another example of how an eating disorder can distort a sufferer's perceptions. Every person is a unique individual. An eating disorder will only hold someone back, not help. If you feel that you are powerless to

Medical professionals, such as your family physician, will help guide you on the road to recovery.

change your habits and attitudes toward food and eating, it is time to ask someone for help. The first step in finding help is acknowledging that you need it.

Often, asking a trusted adult is the best way to get help. Nonetheless, some people do not feel comfortable doing so. As an alternative, somebody who needs help can reach out to the professionals at a local hospital or contact an eating disorder association, such as the NEDA, for information about where to turn. Another good place to start may be with a primary-care doctor. If you suffer from an eating disorder, your doctor will be able to refer you to an eating disorder specialist or advise you about other steps that you can take.

The best way to recover from an eating disorder is by getting professional help. During the course of treatment, someone with an eating disorder will likely be introduced to a few well-trained professionals, including physicians, counselors, dietitians, nutritionists, nurses, and therapists, who are well versed in the best ways to assist someone in his or her situation. These people, along with family members and friends, make up a treatment team.

It is best to avoid fad diets or "secret plans" found on the Internet that promise to help you recover. These plans are often ineffective and can be outright dangerous.

Most important, somebody who has an eating disorder should be involved in choosing a recovery plan.

Fad diets and "detox" regimens are not recovery plans. If you think you may have an eating disorder, seek professional medical help.

Sitting down with his or her doctor or family and discussing what options are available is important. Together, a person with an eating disorder and his or her treatment team can decide which options best fit the situation.

Treatment Options

Recovering from an eating disorder is a multistep process that will likely involve a few different health professionals, including a medical doctor, a nutritionist, and a mental health counselor. Depending upon the situation, treatment may be outpatient, meaning that the person undergoing treatment meets with specialists during the day but lives at home, or treatment may require inpatient care in a hospital or residential care facility. The earlier treatment begins, the less physical and mental damage the eating disorder is likely to do.

Medical Advice

The first step in treatment is to return the body to a physically healthy state. This often means undergoing a thorough medical exam with a family doctor. Depending on the results of that exam, the primary doctor can assemble a team of doctors, therapists, nutritionists, and any other health professionals that can help with the patient's recovery.

A medical exam may uncover critical conditions of the heart, liver, kidneys, brain, skeleton, and muscular,

There are no specific medications that will cure an eating disorder. Recovery from an eating disorder is never as simple as taking a pill. However, there are some medications that may assist in a person's recovery. For example, a doctor may prescribe an antiemetic, which is a medication that is effective against nausea and vomiting, to a person recovering from bulimia. Doctors may also administer electrolytes, which are substances in the body's fluids that help process waste and absorb vitamins and minerals, to restore the balance of these essential chemicals in the body.

Another possibility is that people who are recovering from an eating disorder may feel anxious when attempting to eat healthily again. The National Association of Anorexia Nervosa and Associated Disorders (ANAD) also reports that nearly half of people suffering from an eating disorder also suffer from depression, and some studies suggest that eating disorders are on the spectrum of obsessive-compulsive disorder (OCD). Doctors may use medications to help relieve the symptoms of anxiety, depression, or OCD to assist in the patient's psychological or emotional recovery as well. However, these medications are rarely used alone. They are almost always used in conjunction with other forms of treatment or therapies.

MEDICATION

digestive, or hormonal systems that may need to be addressed before other therapies can begin. The examination can also help the doctor determine if the person needs to be hospitalized for a period of time or

if outpatient treatment is a better option.

If the person is suffering from severe symptoms of a medical crisis, there is a stronger chance that he or she will need to be admitted to a hospital, at least temporarily. This could be due to dehydration, severe malnourishment, an electrolyte imbalance, or in some cases even suicidal thoughts. Somebody with symptoms such as the aforementioned may be given fluids and nutrients through a vein in the arm until he or she is strong enough to eat independently.

For people suffering from anorexia, a health professional will also need to help gradually reintroduce solid foods into the

A thorough medical exam is necessary to reveal underlying physical problems that need to be addressed. The information gathered will also help a doctor put together the best recovery team possible.

body. People who suffer from bulimia may have trained their bodies to throw up after every meal as well. Now, even though they want to get better, in some cases these patients cannot control the urge to vomit after eating. To help them begin to keep food down, a doctor may prescribe an anti-nausea medication.

Nutritional Therapy

By the time they seek treatment, people with an eating disorder may have already damaged their body chemistry to the point it has disturbed the way their brains function. Chemicals in the brain control how people think, feel, and behave. For treatment to be successful, these patients may need to tackle their disordered eating before they can work on the underlying causes of their eating disorder. Dietitians and nutritionists can work with them so they develop healthy eating habits.

Because many people with eating disorders are treated on an outpatient basis, friends and family members are critical to the success of the treatment. They can help by making certain the patient is eating the prescribed foods at the appropriate times. Being watchful and keeping patients busy after meals to distract them and prevent secretive purging may also be helpful. Oftentimes, these friends and family members may feel guilty for monitoring their friend or family member so closely, but their watchful eye is key to the patient's recovery. Once patients are eating healthily, then they are ready to begin a type of treatment known as psychotherapy to help address the underlying causes of their eating disorder.

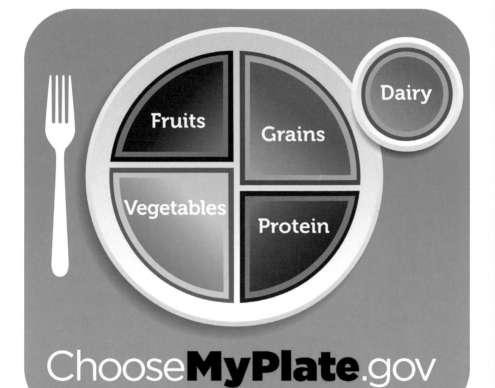

Learning to eat a healthy, well-balanced diet is a key part of the recovery process. A professional nutritionist or dietitian can help develop a nutritional plan customized to a patient's needs.

Psychotherapy

Psychotherapy is a series of techniques that doctors, therapists, and counselors use to treat a psychological, mental, or emotional disorder. People who have an eating disorder may encounter a number of mental health professionals in the course of their treatment. These medical health professionals may include psychiatrists, psychologists, counselors, and therapists. Even though many people confuse what each of these health professionals does, each one plays a unique role in a patient's mental recovery.

A psychiatrist is a medical doctor who specializes in the diagnosis and treatment of mental illnesses. Because psychiatrists are medical doctors, they can write prescriptions for medications or perform medical procedures if they are needed. A psychologist has a doctoral degree in psychology. Psychology is the scientific study of the mind and the way it behaves. A psychologist may work in tandem with a psychiatrist who can provide medical support if necessary but is not able to write prescriptions or perform medical procedures. A mental health counselor has a master's degree in psychology or counseling.

Patients undergoing treatment for an eating disorder may also encounter the terms "therapy" and "counseling." Therapy, which is short for psychotherapy, seeks to uncover a person's patterns of thought and to create an understanding of why those patterns exist. Counseling generally focuses more on a specific issue and ways to cope with or avoid the problem. Therapy and counseling may be used in conjunction with one another to help a patient understand the underlying causes of his or her eating disorder, while at the same time learning strategies and tools that will help him or her deal with unhealthy thoughts and behaviors. Several different types of psychotherapy and counseling may be used in the treatment of an eating disorder. These treatments may include individual, family, or group therapy.

Individual Therapy

Individual therapy involves a one-on-one discussion between a therapist and a patient. By guiding patients through a discussion of their thoughts and feelings, therapists can reassure them and help them see their problems more clearly. Researchers have found that cognitive-behavioral therapy (CBT) is one of the more useful methods of treating an eating disorder. During CBT, a therapist listens to a patient explain how his or her feelings toward food and eating affect his or her life and how it influences the patient's behavior. The therapist then offers suggestions on ways to cope with these feelings and techniques to help change those behaviors.

One technique often employed during CBT for an eating disorder involves keeping a food journal. In a food journal, patients write down what they eat and how they feel while they are eating. The therapist can then help a patient look for patterns in his or her behaviors and feelings

and suggest ways to break those patterns. This technique can help patients understand that when they report feeling "fat," what they may actually be feeling is angry, sad, or disappointed. Understanding that the patient has substituted negative attitudes toward food for bad or overwhelming feelings in general, a therapist can then help the patient develop strategies to cope with the underlying uncomfortable feelings.

Successful CBT helps patients understand why they developed an eating disorder in the first place and teaches them how to change their thought and behavioral patterns. It does this by helping the patient identify triggers, such as

Working with a trained therapist or counselor can help someone with an eating disorder learn to recognize and cope with the thoughts and feelings that trigger his or her disordered eating.

getting a bad grade, family arguments, or encounters with certain people, that may cause the patient to regress into unhealthy eating habits. The next step is assisting the patient in the development of strategies that will help him or her avoid these situations that trigger the eating disorder. In the early stages of treatment, visits to a therapist may occur daily. If treatment progresses successfully, visits may become more spaced out.

Family Therapy

During family therapy, a patient's parents, siblings, or sometimes both join the patient in his or her therapy sessions. Family therapy can help families begin to understand and manage issues within the family that may be contributing to the patient's eating disorder. It can also help family members understand how the patient is feeling and how to help him or her. Family members may even come to realize that they are dealing with milder forms of eating disorders or unhealthy dietary habits themselves. Finally, family therapy can often help begin the healing process in relationships that may have been damaged by the eating disorder.

Group Therapy

During group therapy, a trained therapist leads a group of people dealing with the same issues through a group discussion. Group therapy can help a patient understand and begin to resolve some of the issues that underlie an eating disorder.

A support group is similar to group therapy but usually does not have a mental health professional acting as a facilitator for the discussion. Instead, group leaders may be people who are recovering from an eating disorder themselves. Support groups give people who are struggling with an eating disorder the opportunity to come together with people who have encountered the same, or similar, problems. People in a support group generally share their experiences and encourage one another to continue with their recovery. Support groups can help patients improve their self-esteem and equip them with coping mechanisms that have worked for other people in their situation.

Because they involve discussions of feelings and behavior, the various types of psychotherapy are sometimes referred to as "talk therapy." But not all therapy involves talking. Patients may also encounter art or drama therapies that can help them express their thoughts and feelings in nonverbal ways. Music therapy may help patients overcome issues of self-esteem or fear of failure that may be the underlying causes of their eating disorders by writing or singing songs, beating on a drum, or strumming a guitar. If nonverbal therapies sound interesting to somebody suffering from an eating disorder, or if that person feels more comfortable with these types of therapies, then he or she could ask the treatment team how to find the right kind of therapy.

Scientists are also researching new ways to treat eating disorders. According to an article in the *Huffington Post*

published on March 8, 2013, recent research into deep brain stimulation, which is currently used to help people who suffer from Parkinson's disease and obsessive-compulsive disorder, indicates that the technique may also be useful in people who suffer from anorexia. Deep brain stimulation involves activating different parts of the brain with electrical impulses. The electrical impulses cause the release of serotonin and inhibit the release of cortisol. You may recall that people who develop anorexia often have higher levels of cortisol than people who do not have anorexia. Although deep brain stimulation has not yet been studied as a possible

The support and experiences of other people who have also struggled with eating disorders may help a patient on his or her road to recovery.

treatment for other eating disorders, scientists have identified different areas of the brain that they believe are involved in the compulsion to undereat or overeat.

Many people who have recovered from an eating disorder have reported an overwhelming urge to give up at some point during their treatment. Recovering from an eating disorder is not simple. While recovering from an eating disorder, it is possible that a person will try some therapies that feel like they are not working. But it is crucial not to give up. There are many roads to recovery. Staying involved with treatment will help a patient greatly, and if something does not feel right or if something seems to not be working, the patient should speak up. When a person undergoing treatment expresses to the treatment team the problems with a given therapy, it enables the team to help the person find a better therapy for his or her specific case. With the help of a doctor, family members, and friends, anybody with an eating disorder can break the pattern of disordered eating and make a full recovery.

1. What is a healthy weight for my height and age?

2. What effects have my eating disorder had on my body?

3. What are the different treatment options I could choose?

4. How long will each treatment option take?

5. What foods should I be eating and in what size portions?

6. Are there medications available for my eating disorder, and what are their side effects?

7. What type of exercise would you recommend that I do as I recover, and how frequently?

8. How can I improve my body image and self-esteem?

9. How can I best deal with the emotional issues that led to my eating disorder?

10. How can I find people who will support me?

10 GREAT QUESTIONS TO ASK A TREATMENT SPECIALIST

LONG-TERM RECOVERY

Admitting that food was controlling your life may have been the first step to recovery, but learning how to take back control is a life-long process. People who are recovering from an eating disorder may have to relearn how to eat openly, with others, and not in secret. Or they may need to learn not to control their weight by starvation or purging, but instead by eating reasonable amounts of healthy foods.

Recovering from an eating disorder takes time, patience, and effort. Sometimes there may be physical problems, such as a weakened heart, kidneys, or digestive system, which will need to be coped with as well. Patients may feel anxious, scared, depressed, and overwhelmed. Many relapse into their old habits for comfort because these habits are familiar, but relapsing is unhealthy and will never be a permanent solution. With the help of a treatment team, anybody can learn to overcome these obstacles and live a healthy, happy life.

EATING HEALTHY

People with a healthy relationship with food eat at regular intervals. They eat when they are hungry, and they stop when they are full. The human body needs nutrients in order to function properly. Eating healthy, nutritious food is normal and necessary for the body to get these nutrients. Healthy foods in healthy amounts also help regulate emotions and allow a person to think clearly. Carbohydrates are the body's source of energy. Healthy levels of fats help protect internal organs and

Learning to provide the body with the proper amounts of proteins, fats, fruits, vegetables, and grains is crucial to a healthy relationship with food and weight.

keep the skin from drying out. Proteins help build and repair muscles, and vitamins and minerals generally help the body systems carry out their jobs.

Different foods contain different nutrients. Whole grains, fruits, vegetables, dairy products, and foods that contain protein—such as meat, nuts, eggs, and beans—make up a balanced diet. The body converts the food a person eats into energy. A kilocalorie is the unit for that energy. In common speech, people have shortened the word "kilocalorie" to simply "calorie." On average, a child between the ages of nine and thirteen needs between 1,600 and 2,000 calories a day to develop and grow properly. A teenaged girl needs about 2,000 calories, while a teenaged boy needs between 2,400 and 2,800 calories a day. It should be noted that these numbers are merely averages. A teenager who plays a sport or is very active, for example, will need more calories. If someone tends to be more sedentary, he or she will require fewer calories. A doctor or nutritionist can advise what is the right amount of caloric intake for a given person.

A nutritionist can also help someone learn how to estimate healthy portions and set up a regular eating schedule. A therapist can guide a person toward following his or her appetite rather than emotions when determining the right times to eat. A therapist can also assist that person in developing the skills needed to detach emotions such as guilt, shame, and comfort from food, leaving him or her free to eat only when genuinely hungry. When young adults develop a healthy relationship with food, they can enjoy what they are eating and the people they are eating with, and not worry about the calories being consumed or the possible weight gain or loss they could incur.

During recovery, it is important to remember that fad diets or reliance on diet pills or purging will not help in the long run. Using these methods of weight control won't teach somebody how to eat a healthy, balanced diet— something that will not only guarantee the best weight for a person's body but will also ensure that his or her body is healthy. Instead of going on a fad diet or falling back on other unhealthy behaviors, the wisest decision is to become educated about healthy proteins, fats, fruits, vegetables, and grains. This knowledge, coupled with the guidance of a trained nutritionist on how to recognize healthy portion sizes of these foods, is the best route to a full recovery.

What to Do If You Relapse

An eating disorder is a chronic illness. It takes time to recover, and recovery may not always go smoothly. If you find yourself falling back into old habits, the first thing you should do is forgive yourself for the lapse in judgment. You are learning a new way of living and eating. That is huge! Dwelling on the fact that you have temporarily slipped back into old habits will not help. Instead, speak with a trusted friend, family member, or professional on your treatment team. Acknowledge that you are having a little bit of a problem and ask them to help you get back on track.

Another thing that may assist in recovery is limiting any negative discussions about food, weight, and appearance. If a patient has friends or family members who do not speak positively about these topics, it is in the patient's best interests to ask them to refrain from mentioning these things in his or her presence.

STEPS TO IMPROVING BODY IMAGE

While recovering, it is important to remember that body image is just that—an image. It is how a person imagines his or her body to be, not how it really is. Just as a person with an eating disorder has developed a negative body image, he or she can learn to replace it with a positive one. This may take some practice, but it will be worth it in the end.

Another key aspect to recovery is a person's attitude about himself or herself. People come in all shapes and sizes. Genetics play a big role in body type, and there is only so much a person can do to change the way he or she looks. Those who are recovering from an eating disorder have to learn to appreciate themselves as unique individuals and not compare their body shape with the unrealistic body types portrayed by the media.

One potentially helpful tool is committing to a media "cleanse" during recovery. A media cleanse entails limiting as much media consumption as possible and taking a break from the constant bombardment of images on television and the Internet and

Going on a nature hike is just one fun, healthy way to get away from the influence of visual media. Make a list of the fun things you would like to do.

in movies, magazines, and music videos. At first, this type of cleanse can be for just a few hours. Then it can increase to a full day and then a weekend. Instead of watching television or consuming other forms of visual media, a patient can engage in activities such as reading a book, taking a nature walk, or talking on the phone with a supportive friend. A useful activity at the beginning of such a cleanse is making a list of other fun activities that do not require any sort of media-generated images.

Being surrounded with supportive people can help in recovery from disordered eating, too. If you are recovering from an eating disorder, and the people

BECOME A MEDIA CRITIC

Social pressure from peers and the media can convince young men and women that they cannot be popular and attractive without being thin. For those who are susceptible to developing an eating disorder, as well as those who are trying to recover from one, this pressure can result in unrealistic expectations.

Magazines and commercials advertise the latest weight-loss plans while being plastered with tall, thin supermodels. Movies and television shows perpetuate the same ideal. However, this ideal is not reality. The average female model is 5 foot 11 inches and weighs 120 pounds. The average American woman stands 5 foot 4 inches tall and weighs 140 pounds. It is difficult to ignore these culturally imposed ideals.

Viewers always need to evaluate advertising with a critical eye. Inclusive advertisements do not judge people based solely on their physical appearance, and they show people with a healthy variety of sizes and shapes. They do not depict larger people with negative characteristics, while ascribing only good characteristics to thin people. Responsible advertisements do not ridicule people who are overweight, and they do not glamorize stories and images of people dieting. Instead, they show people eating balanced meals as part of a healthy lifestyle.

Remember, you are not powerless against these messages. You can decide to become a media critic. Be a free thinker and reject the unrealistic images portrayed in the media. As a consumer, anybody has the right to speak up, including you. If you do not like what you see in your favorite magazine, write a letter to the editor. If they continue to portray unrealistic body images, speak with your wallet and stop buying that magazine. There are positive role models, such as Jennifer Lawrence, who told *Elle* magazine in a December 2013 interview: "I'm never going to starve myself for a part. I don't want little girls to be like, 'Oh, I want to look like Katniss, so I'm going to skip dinner'... I was trying to get my body to look fit and strong—not thin and underfed." By supporting positive role models and the magazines and advertisers that use them, a consumer also sends a strong message to the media.

around you are making a big deal out of physical appearance, you do not have to go along with them. You can change the subject or leave the room. By making a pledge to speak out against the mentality that appearance is the most important ingredient for happiness and success in life, someone in recovery can truly commit to changing his or her environment and approach to body image. It requires courage and commitment, but with determination, anybody can change and affect the influences around him or her.

Once a healthy weight is reached, a person's self-worth and positive self-image should have nothing to do with a number on the scale. Whenever the urge to check the scale comes up, a healthy person can simply substitute that urge with a different activity that he or she enjoys. If you are overcoming or have overcome an eating disorder, concentrate on who you really are inside and focus on the goals you would like to achieve—goals that have nothing to do with food or weight. Patients

Surround yourself with fun, positive people. Make a pact with your friends to speak and act only with loving kindness toward one another.

both in recovery or who have already completed treatment should focus on adding at least one pleasurable, playful act to their day every day. Everyone deserves it!

Focus on the fun of physical activity, not how many calories it will burn. Try salsa dancing, a yoga class, or hula hooping just because they sound like something that would be fun to do. Vow to wear that super outfit today, not when there's a special occasion or when you drop a few more pounds. If you like it, wear it. Feeling good is a special occasion.

When negative thoughts or emotions arise, it is important to stop. It is surprisingly easy to take a few deep breaths, acknowledge a negative thought or feeling, and then simply let it go. Think of it as a small bird that you release, and as you watch the bird fly away, think of a positive thought to replace it. The negative chatter that somebody hears in his or her head is like a habit that can be changed one thought at a time.

Surround yourself with things you love and compliment yourself every day. Some days it may feel hard to come up with something nice to say about yourself. On days like that, acknowledge that you are trying and that you are doing the best you can. Self-kindness is another crucial quality in taking back control of your life.

Feed your body what you would feed someone you love. Make a commitment to take care of your body. Notice the sensations in your body without judgment and think of your body with loving kindness. Listen to and respect its needs. Eat when you are hungry. Do something else that makes you happy when you are not. Make it your goal to be healthy, not thin.

HEALTHY WAYS TO COPE

For every patient, a large part of the recovery process will involve learning healthy ways in which to express his or her feelings. A recovery team can help in finding activities that do not involve food—activities that can help alleviate anxious or unhappy thoughts. These hobbies might include writing in a journal, drawing or painting a picture, going for a run, or calling a supportive friend.

If you are in the recovery process and you feel the urge to fall back into destructive habits, you should discuss these feelings with a member of your treatment team. Distractions such as walking the dog, taking a bubble bath, or reading a favorite book can help push negative thoughts out of your mind. Remember that, in the long run, the behaviors associated with your eating disorder did not make you happy and vow to discover new behaviors that do. Pay attention to what makes you feel good and do more of that.

Set yourself up for success, not failure. Take calorie-counting apps off your phone and other devices. Focus on eating the healthy, balanced diet prescribed for you by your doctor or nutritionist. Most important, love yourself for who you are now, not for who you wish you could be. Give yourself credit every time you resist the urge to skip a meal, purge after eating, or avoid eating unhealthy foods. Take pride in listening to and taking care of your body.

Practice valuing your own thoughts and opinions and do not put yourself down. Do not let others put you down either. If somebody in recovery has friends who indulge in "fat talk," he or she should have a talk with

Build a support system of friends who care about who you are, not what you look like. This will help you feel more confident with a healthy body and mind.

them. By explaining that what they are doing makes him or her feel bad, the friends of somebody recovering from an eating disorder are more likely to choose to banish negative self-talk when they are around that person. Together, that person and his or her friends can support and encourage each other. They can even make it a challenge to help build each other's self-esteem instead of tearing it down, focusing on inner qualities such as kindness, generosity, or sensitivity, as well as artistic or academic achievements, rather than outer appearance.

Finally, if you are trying to recover from an eating disorder, you should understand that no one is perfect, and you don't have to be either. Do not compare yourself with the people you see in advertisements, magazines, television shows, and movies. Focus on being the best you that you can be.

Your treatment team can help you learn to recognize people and events that tend to trigger your eating disorder and to develop strategies to avoid those people and situations as much as possible. Do not be afraid to ask for help if you need it and accept the support that those who care about you try to give.

Doing so will not only help you recover, it will also help repair relationships that may have suffered under the weight of your illness.

One of the key things to remember is that you do not have to do this alone. There are people who have struggled with eating disorders and recovered. With the support of your treatment team, you can go on to lead a long, healthy life free of unhealthy eating habits, too.

Take good care of yourself. Eat quality food in healthy amounts. Get enough sleep and treat yourself with compassion. Focus on being healthy, moving your body, feeling strong, and having fun. You can do it and you are worth the effort!

Enlist the help of family and friends to make every meal a fun, healthy, and happy experience. You will all reap the benefits.

GLOSSARY

amenorrhea The absence of a monthly menstrual cycle in women who have reached puberty.

anorexia athletica Also known as hypergymnasia, an eating disorder characterized by the obsessive need to exercise vigorously.

anorexia nervosa An eating disorder characterized by self-starvation and extreme weight loss.

binge To consume excessive amounts of calories in a short period of time.

binge eating disorder An eating disorder characterized by the uncontrollable urge to eat large amounts of food in short periods of time.

body image A mental picture of how a person feels he or she appears to other people.

bulimia nervosa An eating disorder characterized by periods of binge eating followed by purging, commonly by vomiting or the use of laxatives.

dehydration An excessive loss of water from the body.

depression A feeling of hopelessness and inadequacy that lasts for long periods of time.

diuretic A medication that promotes urine production.

electrolyte Charged particle necessary for many of the reactions that take place in the body.

genetic Relating to characteristics that are passed down from parent to offspring.

hormone Chemical messenger that signals a variety of cells to perform specific functions in the body.

lanugo A dense layer of hair that grows in the absence of a fat layer to keep the body warm.

laxative A medication that promotes the elimination of feces.

metabolism The chemical reactions that occur within the body to sustain life.

nutrients Chemicals present in food that are necessary to sustain life.

obesity A condition characterized by having too much body fat.

osteoporosis A condition in which the bones become brittle and easily break.

predisposition A liability or tendency to suffer from a condition or behave a certain way.

psychiatrist A medical doctor who specializes in mental illnesses and their treatment.

psychologist An expert or specialist with a doctoral degree in psychology.

purge The removal of food or the elimination of calories from the body.

self-esteem A person's sense of self-worth or self-respect.

FOR MORE INFORMATION

Academy for Eating Disorders (AED)
111 Deer Lake Road, Suite 100
Deerfield, IL 60015
(847) 498-4274
Website: https://www.aedweb.org
The AED is a professional organization for doctors, therapists, and other health care professionals who are involved in eating disorder research, education, treatment, and prevention.

Alliance for Eating Disorders Awareness
1649 Forum Place, #2
West Palm Beach, FL 33401
(866) 662-1235
Website: http://www.allianceforeatingdisorders.com
The Alliance for Eating Disorders Awareness provides outreach and education programs designed to prevent eating disorders by promoting a positive body image.

Binge Eating Disorder Association (BEDA)
637 Emerson Place
Severna Park, MD 21146
(855) 855-2332
Website: http://bedaonline.com
BEDA is committed to working with doctors and other professionals to develop the best treatments for binge eating disorder as well as helping people who suffer from the disorder get the treatment they need.

Canadian Mental Health Association (CMHA)

1110-151 Slater Street
Ottawa, ON K1P 5H3
Canada
(416) 979-7948
Website: http://www.cmha.ca

The CMHA promotes mental health for all Canadians suffering from a mental illness, including those with eating disorders, through advocacy, education, research, and service.

Eating Disorders Coalition (EDC)

720 7th Street NW, Suite 300
Washington, DC 20001
(202) 543-9570
Website: http://www.eatingdisorderscoalition.org

The EDC advocates for the recognition and fiscal support of eating disorder prevention programs at the state and federal level.

National Association of Anorexia Nervosa and Associated Disorders (ANAD)

750 East Diehl Road, #127
Naperville, IL 60563
(630) 577-1333
Website: http://www.anad.org

ANAD seeks to support, educate, and connect people with eating disorders with people who can help them. Online help and a helpline are available at its website.

National Association for Males with Eating Disorders (NAMED)

118 Palm Drive, #11

Naples, FL 34112

(877) 780-0080

Website: http://namedinc.org

NAMED provides online support group discussion forums for men and boys struggling with eating disorders as well as those who care about them.

National Eating Disorders Association (NEDA)

165 West 46th Street, Suite 402

New York, NY 10036

(212) 575-6200

Helpline: (800) 931-2237

Website: http://www.nationaleatingdisorders.org

The NEDA offers information about eating disorders, online eating disorder screening, and online help, as well as a toll-free, confidential helpline.

National Eating Disorder Information Centre

ES 7-421, 200 Elizabeth Street

Toronto, ON M5G 2C4

Canada

(416) 340-4156

Helpline: (866) 633-4220

Website: http://www.nedic.ca

The National Eating Disorder Information Centre offers educational information about eating disorders, runs prevention and awareness campaigns, and provides support for finding treatment options available in Canada. It also offers a free self-esteem and body image curriculum for teachers at the website www.beyondimages.ca.

WEBSITES

Because of the changing nature of Internet links, Rosen Publishing has developed an online list of websites related to the subject of this book. This site is updated regularly. Please use the following link to access the list:

http://www.rosenlinks.com/411/Eati

FOR FURTHER READING

Ambrose, Marylou, and Veronica Deisler.
    *Investigating Eating Disorders (Anorexia,
    Bulimia, and Binge Eating): Real Facts from
    Real Lives.* Berkeley Heights, NJ: Enslow
    Publishers, 2010.
Anderson, Laurie Halse. *Wintergirls.* New York, NY:
    Viking, 2009.
Arnold, Carrie, and B. Timothy Walsh. *Next to
    Nothing: A Firsthand Account of One Teenager's
    Experience with an Eating Disorder.* New York,
    NY: Oxford University Press, 2007.
Brinkerhoff, Shirley. *Eating Disorders* (State of Mental
    Illness and Its Therapy). Broomall, PA: Mason
    Crest, 2014.
Costin, Carolyn. *8 Keys to Recovery from an Eating
    Disorder: Effective Strategies from Therapeutic
    Practice and Personal Experience.* New York, NY:
    W. W. Norton & Company, 2011.
Danowski, Debbie. *Why Can't My Child Stop Eating?:
    A Guide to Helping Your Child Overcome
    Emotional Overeating.* Las Vegas, NV: Central
    Recovery Press, 2013.
Espejo, Roman. *Eating Disorders* (Opposing Viewpoints).
    San Diego, CA: Greenhaven Press, 2012.
Foran, Racquel. *Living with Eating Disorders.*
    Minneapolis, MN: ABDO Publishing Co., 2014.

Friedman, Lauri S., ed. *Body Image* (Introducing Issues with Opposing Viewpoints). San Diego, CA: Greenhaven Press, 2012.

Gerdes, Louise. *The Culture of Beauty* (Opposing Viewpoints). Detroit, MI: Greenhaven Press, 2013.

Gillard, Arthur, ed. *Anorexia and Bulimia* (Perspectives on Diseases and Disorders). San Diego, CA: Greenhaven Press, 2013.

Gillard, Arthur. *Eating Disorders* (Issues That Concern You). San Diego, CA: Greenhaven Press, 2010.

Grabau, Melissa. *The Yoga of Food: Wellness from the Inside Out*. Woodbury, MN: Llewellyn Publications, 2014.

Haerens, Margaret. *Eating Disorders* (Global Viewpoints). San Diego, CA: Greenhaven Press, 2012.

Hillstrom, Kevin, ed. *Eating Disorders* (Nutrition and Health). Farmington Hills, MI: Lucent Books, 2012.

Iorizzo, Carrie. *Eating Disorders* (Straight Talk About). New York, NY: Crabtree Publishing Co., 2013.

Lankford, Ronald D., Jr. *Body Image* (Hot Topics). San Diego, CA: Lucent Books, 2010.

Metzger, Lois. *A Trick of the Light*. New York, NY: Balzer & Bray, 2013.

Owens, Peter. *Teens, Health & Obesity*. Philadelphia, PA: Mason Crest, 2013.

Radey, Anna, ed. *I've Got This Friend Who: Advice for Teens and Their Friends on Alcohol, Drugs,*

Eating Disorders, Risky Behavior, and More.
Center City, MN: Hazelden, 2010.

Schab, Lisa. *The Bulimia Workbook for Teens:
Activities to Help You Stop Bingeing and Purging.*
Oakland, CA: New Harbinger Publications,
Inc., 2010.

Schab, Lisa. *The Self-Esteem Workbook for Teens:
Activities to Help You Build Confidence and
Achieve Your Goals.* Oakland, CA: New
Harbinger Publications, Inc., 2013.

Shahan, Sherry. *Skin and Bones.* Chicago, IL: Albert
Whitman & Company, 2014.

Smith, Rita, Vanessa Baish, Edward Willett, and
Stephanie Watson. *Self-Image and Eating
Disorders.* New York, NY: Rosen Publishing
Group, 2012.

Smolin, Lori, and Mary Grosvenor. *Nutrition and
Eating Disorders.* New York, NY: Chelsea House
Publications, 2010.

BIBLIOGRAPHY

BBC News. "Health: Brain Chemicals May Cause Bulimia." October 14, 1998. Retrieved February 17, 2014 (http://news.bbc.co.uk/2/hi/health/192727.stm).

BBC News. "Health: Genetic Clues to Eating Disorders." January 21, 1999. Retrieved February 17, 2014 (http://news.bbc.co.uk/2/hi/health/259226.stm).

Bidwell, Allie. "Researchers Find Genes Linked to High Risk of Eating Disorders." *U.S. News & World Report*, October 8, 2013. Retrieved February 17, 2014 (http://www.usnews.com/news/articles/2013/10/08/researchers-find-genes-linked-to-high-risk-of-eating-disorders).

Binge Eating Disorder Association. "Understanding BED." Retrieved February 17, 2014 (http://bedaonline.com/understanding-bed/#.UwPC8HlhVuo).

Blalock, Meghan. "12 Celebrities Who Famously Battled Eating Disorders and Won." StyleCaster, January 6, 2014. Retrieved February 17, 2014 (http://www.stylecaster.com/celebrities-eating-disorders).

Carlton, Pamela, and Deborah Ashin. *Take Charge of Your Child's Eating Disorder: A Physician's Step-by-Step Guide to Defeating Anorexia and Bulimia.* New York, NY: Marlowe & Co, 2007.

Curtin, Elise. "New Year May Bring New Treatment for Eating Issues." GoodTherapy.org, December 31, 2013. Retrieved February 17, 2014 (http://www

.goodtherapy.org/blog/new-year-may-bring-new
-treatment-for-eating-issues).

Herzong, David, Debra Franko, and Pat Cable.
*Unlocking the Mysteries of Eating Disorders: A
Life-Saving Guide to Your Child's Treatment and
Recovery.* New York, NY: McGraw-Hill, 2008.

Kandel, Johanna. *Life Beyond Your Eating Disorder:
Reclaim Yourself, Regain Your Health, Recover
for Good.* New York, NY: Harlequin, 2010.

Kindelan, Katie. "Jennifer Lawrence 'Considered
a Fat Actress.'" ABC News, November 8,
2012. Retrieved February 17, 2014 (http://
abcnews.go.com/blogs/entertainment/2012/11/
jennifer-lawrence-considered-a-fat-actress).

Kotz, Deborah. "How Much Exercise Is Too Much?"
Boston Globe, August 5, 2013. Retrieved
February 17, 2014 (http://www.bostonglobe
.com/lifestyle/health-wellness/2013/08/04/can
-too-much-exercise-harm-heart-and-shorten
-your-life/VLlkXGBN9f1t6raYmUSuPJ/
story.html).

Mansour, Iris. "'Thinspiration' Packages Eating
Disorders as a Lifestyle Choice." Mashable,
December 6, 2013. Retrieved February 17, 2014
(http://mashable.com/2013/12/05/thinspiration).

Miller, Hilary. "Celebrities Speak Out Against
Photoshop." *Huffington Post*, January 10, 2014.
Retrieved February 17, 2014 (http://www
.huffingtonpost.com/2014/01/10/celebrities

-photoshop_n_4576398.html?utm_hp_ref=
entertainment&ir=Entertainment#sl
ide=3307594).

Mullins, Jenna. "Bikini Bridge: Everything You
Need to Know About This Horrible (and Fake)
New Body Trend." E! Online, January 10, 2014.
Retrieved February 17, 2014 (http://www.eonline
.com/news/497785/bikini-bridge-everything-you
-need-to-know-about-this-horrible-and-fake-new
-body-trend).

National Eating Disorders Association. "General
Information." Retrieved February 17, 2014
(http://www.nationaleatingdisorders.org/general
-information).

National Institute of Arthritis and Musculoskeletal
and Skin Diseases. "What People with Anorexia
Nervosa Need to Know About Osteoporosis."
January 2012. Retrieved February 17, 2014
(http://www.niams.nih.gov/Health_Info/Bone/
Osteoporosis/Conditions_Behaviors/anorexia_
nervosa.asp).

Nature World News. "Social Networking Sites
Promoting Eating Disorders." October 5, 2013.
Retrieved February 17, 2014 (http://www
.natureworldnews.com/articles/4334/20131005/
social-networking-sites-promoting-eating
-disorders.htm).

Paul, Annie Murphy. "Baby's First Diet Pill." New
York Times, August 5, 2007. Retrieved February

17, 2014 (http://www.nytimes.com/2007/08/05/ magazine/05wwln-idealab-t.html?_r=0).

Shepphird, Sari Fine. *100 Questions & Answers About Anorexia Nervosa.* Sudbury, MA: Jones and Bartlett Publishers, 2010.

Stein, Ricki. "Cathy Rigby Shares Her Nightmare of Bulimia, Anorexia." *Morning Call*, June 7, 1988. Retrieved February 17, 2014 (http://articles .mcall.com/1988-06-07/news/2627062_1_cathy -rigby-bulimia-anorexia).

Vecsey, George. "Cathy Rigby, Unlike Peter, Did Grow Up." *New York Times*, December 19, 1990. Retrieved February 17, 2014 (http://www.nytimes .com/1990/12/19/sports/sports-of-the-times-cathy -rigby-unlike-peter-did-grow-up.html).

INDEX

A

Abdul, Paula, 11
abuse, 27
alcoholism, 27
amenorrhea, 44, 49, 52
anorexia athletica, 20, 52
anorexia nervosa, 8–12,
    14, 15, 16, 18, 20,
    40, 52
  death and, 11, 12, 41
  health complications of,
    41–46
  possible causes of, 10,
    25, 75
  and social media, 35
  statistics on, 11–12, 41
  symptoms of, 8, 10,
    41–44
  treatment, 65–66, 75
anxiety, 4, 7, 10, 14, 23, 30,
    56, 63, 78, 89
Apple, Fiona, 11
art therapy, 73
athletes, and eating disor-
    ders, 27, 30, 52–53

B

"bikini bridge," 35
binge eating disorder, 12–14,
    20, 38
  health complications of,
    46–49

statistics on, 14
  symptoms of, 12, 14
Binge Eating Disorder
    Association (BEDA), 14
biological causes of eating
    disorders, 23–26
black and white thinking, 29
blood pressure, high, 48, 49
body dysmorphic disorder, 32
body image, 30–33, 39
  distorted, 15, 30–32
  improving, 82–88
bulimia nervosa, 14–18, 20,
    40, 63
  health complications of,
    49–55
  possible cause of, 25
  and social media, 35
  statistics on, 16
  symptoms of, 14–15, 16, 18
  treatment, 66
bullying, 10, 38

C

caloric intakes, recom-
    mended, 80
Carpenter, Karen, 11, 53
celebrities and eating
    disorders, 11
chemical imbalances,
    23–26, 56
cholesterol, 48

ABOUT THE AUTHOR

Kristi Lew is a professional K–12 educational writer with a background in biochemistry and genetics. She has authored several important guides for young adults on health, nutrition, and well-being, including *The Truth About Oxycodone and Other Narcotics* and *Food Poisoning: E. coli and the Food Supply*. With a background as a teacher of high school science, Lew has seen firsthand the damage eating disorders can do to young lives. She feels strongly that education and treatment can empower young people to regain control over their eating habits and reclaim their lives.

PHOTO CREDITS

Cover, p. 1 Peter Bernik/Shutterstock.com; p. 5 Tomaz Levstek/E+/Getty Images; p. 9 MachineHeadz/E+/Getty Images; p. 13 Alo Ceballos/FilmMagic/Getty Images; pp. 16–17 Photodisc/Thinkstock; pp. 18–19 © SuperStock/Alamy; pp. 21, 31 Glow Wellness/Getty Images; p. 24 snapgalleria/Shutterstock.com; p. 26 Meletios/Shutterstock.com; pp. 28–29 Pixland/Thinkstock; pp. 36–37 Hitoshi Nishimura/The Image Bank/Getty Images; pp. 42–43 Jack Hollingsworth/Photodisc/Thinkstock; p. 45 BSIP/Science Source; p. 47 moodboard/Thinkstock; pp. 50–51 John Bavosi/Science Source; pp. 54–55 © Jeff Greenberg/Alamy; pp. 58–59 Catherine Yeulet/iStock/Thinkstock; p. 61 © AP Images; pp. 64–65 © iStockophoto.com/AlexRaths; p. 67 USDA; pp. 70–71 alexsokolov/iStock/Thinkstock; pp. 74–75 © iStockphoto.com/Steve Debenport; pp. 78–79 © iStockphoto.com/robynmac; p. 83 Andersen Ross/Blend Images/Thinkstock; pp. 86–87 Fuse/Thinkstock; pp. 90–91 loooby/iStock/Thinkstock; pp. 92–93 monkeybusinessimages/iStock/Thinkstock.

Designer: Les Kanturek; Photo Researcher: Amy Feinberg